Bibliographical Series
of Supplements to 'British Book News'
on Writers and Their Work

GENERAL EDITOR
Bonamy Dobrée

ROBERT BROWNING
From the marble bust of 1886 by his son R. W. B. Browning at Balliol College, Oxford
(Reproduced by courtesy of the Master and Fellows of Balliol College, Oxford)

BROWNING

by
JOHN BRYSON

PUBLISHED FOR
THE BRITISH COUNCIL
and the NATIONAL BOOK LEAGUE
by LONGMANS, GREEN & CO.

LONGMANS, GREEN & CO. LTD.
6 & 7 Clifford Street, London W.1
Thibault House, Thibault Square, Cape Town
605–611 Lonsdale Street, Melbourne, C.1

LONGMANS, GREEN & CO. INC.
119 West 40th Street, New York 18

LONGMANS, GREEN & CO.
20 Cranfield Road, Toronto 16

ORIENT LONGMANS PRIVATE LTD.
Calcutta   Bombay   Madras
Delhi   Hyderabad   Dacca

First published in 1959
© John Bryson, 1959

Printed in Great Britain by Unwin Brothers Limited
Woking and London

CONTENTS

¶ ROBERT BROWNING was born at Camberwell on 7 May, 1812. He died in Venice on 12 December, 1889.

ROBERT BROWNING

I

INTRODUCTION

A MARKED revival of interest in Victorian poetry has taken place during recent years. Critical texts are being established and the great figures are being re-examined, now that time has set their work in perspective and removed them from the immediate praise or blame of their contemporaries. Tennyson, Arnold, Rossetti, and lesser poets than these have all stood the test of revaluation and in different ways have come into their own. Judgement on Meredith and Swinburne is in suspense; Browning remains a special and interesting case. No one can mention Victorian poetry without thinking of him; an outstanding figure in his own day he still dominates the scene along with Tennyson. These twin mountain peaks out-top the rest, but Browning now attracts the fewer climbers. The going is hard and only intrepid spirits attempt the ascent. His harsh and craggy landscape seems, as we approach it, not unlike the grim country through which Childe Roland fought his way to the Dark Tower. Tennyson is less of a challenge; his gentler slopes invite reflection and repose instead of a tough and breathless climb. Such is our general impression of the two poets and it needs correction, or at least reconsideration, as far as Browning is concerned. It is the purpose of this essay to show that the time has come to re-read him, and that when the effort is made, or even half made, the rewards he offers are great.

The neglect into which he has fallen is in part a reaction from the over-zealous worship accorded by earnest members of the early Browning Societies who concentrated on the poet's message at the expense of his poetry. Both they and their hero have been wittily caricatured by Max Beerbohm in *The Poets' Corner*. In part also it springs from a misunderstanding like that which often leads to the under-rating of

Scott; certain 'jolly' poems like *Hervé Riel* and *How they brought the Good News from Ghent to Aix*, which are read for duty or pleasure in youth, do not suggest that their author is going to be the right poet for more sophisticated years. But in the main the neglect springs from a fear of Browning's difficulty of style and obscurity of thought.

A poet who has only a message to proclaim ceases to be a poet and becomes a preacher. Browning is indeed a moralist but he seldom preaches; he is too humble and human for that. He believed that the world contains much more good than ill, and he was not afraid to proclaim that belief in assured and sometimes strident tones. He was confident in an age when many were unsure, but the faith and hope which remained unshaken to the end were not achieved without trial, doubt, and self-examination. He is not the mere hearty optimist that he is so often supposed to be, for few poets have had a deeper understanding of human frailty and failure. He is certainly not an easy poet, but the difficulty does not lie in the abstruse nature of his thought which is usually comprehensible enough. It lies in a highly individual manner of expression and in a quick, abrupt way of thinking which does make special demands on the reader. In a letter to Ruskin, who had complained of his bewilderment over *Men and Women*, Browning makes a revealing comment on the nature of his poetry:

> We don't read poetry in the same way, by the same law; it is too clear. I cannot begin writing poetry till my imaginary reader has conceded licences to me which you demur at altogether. I *know* that I don't make out my conception by my language; all poetry being a putting of the infinite within the finite. You would have me paint it all plain out, which can't be. . . . You ought, I think, to keep pace with the thought tripping from ledge to ledge of my 'glaciers', as you call them; not stand poking your alpenstock into the holes and demonstrating that no foot could have stood there:—suppose it sprang over there? In *prose* you may criticize so—because that is the absolute representation of portions of truth, what chronicling is to history—but in asking for more *ultimates*

you must accept less *mediates*, nor expect that a Druid stone-circle will be traced for you with as few breaks to the eye as the North Crescent and South Crescent that go together so cleverly in many a suburb.

And then he goes on to comment on his 'little song' about Hobbs and Nobbs, i.e. the short poem *Popularity* which asks 'What porridge had John Keats?' and leaves the reader to find the answer. In fact he moves swiftly and often erratically, and he asks us to follow and keep pace.

'The diction is harsh, the rhymes uncertain and the numbers unpleasing'; what Dr. Johnson said of *Lycidas* might well seem to apply with more justice to Browning. Eccentric and extravagant rhymes, a diction both colloquial and learned, abrupt rhythms, and rough handling of the lesser part of speech—these are the features his parodists have readily seized on. But these are only one aspect of Browning; when he is writing thus it is usually in character, and there is dramatic excuse. He knew full well that 'song's our art', and in the short poem '*Transcendentalism*', which is a self-criticism, he contrasts the poet who would merely speak his naked thoughts 'instead of draping them in sights and sounds' with another who:

> with a 'look you!' vents a brace of rhymes,
> And in there breaks the sudden rose herself
> Over us, under, round us every side.

Writing in that mood he gives us his greatest things—the silvery harmonies of *Andrea del Sarto*, the passionate invocation which dedicates the *Ring and the Book*, and the great courageous sweep of *Prospice*.

Browning is a learned poet; he read widely both in the high-ways and the by-ways of literature, history, and thought, and forgot little that he read. He had also more than an amateur interest in painting and music. He draws on all this knowledge for the wealth of reference and illustration with which his poetry is loaded. His erudition is not mere intellectual snobbery and display of book learning; it is there because these things were real to him and ready for use. The point of an obscure allusion may often escape anyone less well read than himself, and it is not always worth pursuing for he sometimes over-reached himself. In the main, however, the wide range of reference is but another licence the reader is ready to concede as soon as he has realized how apt and enriching a seemingly remote allusion can be; and that is something he realizes increasingly the better he gets to know Browning. It is, for example, the painter Carlo Maratta who comes with the crowd to make a sketch of the angelic head of the dying Pompilia. Maratta, a minor and now forgotten Roman artist, but just the right man for that time and place: it is touches like this that liven Browning's historical backgrounds and give them depth.

Both Tennyson and Arnold are renowned as exquisite observers of the natural English scene. Browning may lack their verbal magic but he too has his contribution to make to nature poetry, and at its best that contribution is hardly inferior to theirs. He writes of friends:

> Who, arm in arm, deserve the warm
> Moon-births and the long evening ends.[1]

Of young love and summer in an English lane:

> Your ghost will walk, you lover of trees
>   (If loves remain)
> By a corn-field side a-flutter with poppies.
> Hark, those two in the hazel coppice—
> A boy and a girl, if the good fates please,
>   Making love, say—
>   The happier they!
> Draw yourself up from the light of the moon,
> And let them pass, as they will too soon,
>   With the bean-flowers' boon
>   And the blackbird's tune,
>   And May, and June![2]

He catches the tang of an autumn morning;

[1] *May and Death.*   [2] *'De Gustibus—.'*

Oh, good gigantic smile, o' the brown old earth,
  This autumn morning! How he sets his bones
To bask i' the sun, and thrusts out knees and feet
For the ripple to run over in its mirth;
  Listening the while, where on the heap of stones
The white breast of the sea-lark twitters sweet.[1]

Above all he is supreme in his pictures of Italy, the country
he loved in youth, where he spent the happy married years of
middle-life, and to which he returned in old age to die. Asolo,
Florence, the Apennines, the Roman Campagna, the heat and
colour of the Neapolitan south—all its aspects are recorded.
The scirocco blows through *The Englishman in Italy*:

Hark, the quick, whistling pelt of the olives
  Which, thick in one's track,
Tempt the stranger to pick up and bite them,
  Tho' not yet half black!
How the old twisted olive trunks shudder,
  The medlars let fall
Their hard fruit, and brittle great fig-trees
  Snap off, figs and all,—
For here comes the whole of the tempest!
  No refuge, but creep
Back again to my side and my shoulder,
  And listen or sleep.

The noise and movement and colour of Italian life depicted
in *Up at a Villa,—Down in the City* are as fresh as when the
picture was painted a hundred years ago. Browning used
his eyes and ears, and he loved the country and the people
among whom he had settled:

Italy, my Italy!
Queen Mary's saying serves for me—
  (When fortune's malice
  Lost her—Calais)—
Open my heart and you will see
Graved inside of it, 'Italy'.
Such lovers old are I and she;
So it always was, so shall ever be![2]

[1] *Among the Rocks.*   [2] *'De Gustibus—.'*

II

LIFE

Robert Browning was born at Camberwell on the outskirts of London on 7 May, 1812. His father was a senior clerk in the Bank of England, a cultivated man who was by nature more of the quiet scholar than ambitious business man. In his son's words: 'He might have been a great man had he cared a bit about it.' This sympathetic, well-read parent encouraged his son's talent, and played an intelligent part in his education. In a poem of his old age the poet gives us a happy glimpse of how he was introduced to Greek story in nursery days:

> My Father was a scholar and knew Greek.
> When I was five years old, I asked him once
> 'What do you read about?'
>   'The siege of Troy.'
> 'What is a siege and what is Troy?'
>   Whereat
> He piled up chairs and tables for a town,
> Set me a-top for Priam, called our cat
> Helen, enticed away from home (he said)
> By wicked Paris, who couched somewhere close
> Under the footstool, being cowardly. . . .
> This taught me who was who and what was what:
> So far I rightly understood the case
> At five years old: a huge delight it proved
> And still proves—thanks to that instructor sage
> My Father.[1]

His mother, whom Carlyle described as 'the true type of Scottish gentlewoman', brought her son up in an atmosphere of sincere Evangelical piety, and implanted in him the love of music, and delight in a garden which were her own special pleasures. Camberwell was then a country suburb, and a green half-hour's walk away was Dulwich with its woods and gypsies, and the picture-gallery which

[1] *Development.*

early opened the boy's eyes to the pleasures of painting. Like more than one other Victorian poet Browning was fortunate in his early surroundings. All his life he remained devoted to his parents and to his sister, their only other child. The influence of this happy uncramped home-life can be felt in the spirit of confidence which runs throughout his work.

Except for a short period of attendance at the newly opened University of London in 1828 Browning had little formal education after he left school at the age of fourteen. He worked with tutors, and had the run of his father's ample library, and every opportunity was given him for physical and mental development at home. He was no recluse; enduring friendships were made in these early years, there were excursions to the theatre where he saw Kean act, and in due course came opportunities for travel. When he was twenty-two, through the help of an uncle in the Rothschild banking firm, he paid a two months' visit to Russia which he remembered in after years when he came to write *Ivan Ivanovitch*. Four years later, in 1838, he had his first experience of Italy with a visit to Asolo and Venice, and that bore fruit in *Sordello* and *Pippa Passes*. In 1844 he was in Italy again, staying in Naples and Rome, and on the voyage he wrote the well-known lines *Home Thoughts from the Sea*. Then in 1864 he settled with his wife in the country of his adoption for the fourteen happy years of his married life.

This is to anticipate. When the time came to settle on a career Browning chose to be a poet, and his indulgent parents (on whom he remained dependent till his marriage) did not offer serious opposition. *Pauline*, his first poem, appeared in 1833, his aunt paying for its publication; it was noticed but did not sell a single copy. *Paracelus*, which followed in 1835, drew praise from Wordsworth and made him new friends in literary circles, including the actor-manager Macready. The latter's suggestion that Browning should write a play for him fired the young poet with an ambition to make his career as a popular playwright, an aim which he pursued doggedly, but with little tangible success, for the next eight years. No more than Tennyson was he by nature a writer for the stage. His dramatic attempts from *Strafford* (1837) to *Luria* (1846) were not, however, all wasted effort; practice in play-writing led to the discovery of where his special dramatic talent lay—in the study of the single character presented in monologue form.

Sordello, the long poem on which he had been working for four years, appeared in 1840. This notoriously incomprehensible story of a dimly realized troubadour world did little to advance his reputation with the small public who already knew him. Then followed the hard years which test a young writer's belief in himself, and Browning's self-confidence survived the trial. From 1841 to 1846 he issued his plays and poems (at his father's expense) in a series of shilling pamphlets entitled *Bells and Pomegranates*, the eight numbers of which are now a high bibliographical rarity. The characteristically obscure title, referring to the embroidered hem of the Hebrew High-Priests' garment,[1] was meant to symbolize the two elements he was striving to combine in his poetry—music with discoursing, poetry with thought; but that can hardly have been clear till he explained it, thanks to the protests of Miss Barrett, in the final issue. In these booklets, which start with *Pippa Passes* and include the *Dramatic Romances and Lyrics*, his true powers begin to emerge. The outlines are firmer, there is a maturing grasp of real people, and the wide range of his historical imagination becomes evident. Readers whose interest had survived *Sordello* could recognize a new voice, and among them was Elizabeth Barrett, when the poems reached her sick room in Wimpole Street. She expressed her admiration in *Lady Geraldine's Courtship* by linking the new name with those of Wordsworth and Tennyson:

> Or from Browning some pomegranate which if cut deep down the middle,
> Shows a heart within blood-tinctured of a veined humanity.

[1] Exodus xxviii. 33–4.

This was critical appreciation at last, and when Browning read it he wrote to his admirer at the suggestion of John Kenyon, a loyal friend of them both. 'I love your verses with all my heart, dear Miss Barrett . . . I do, as I say love these books with all my heart—and I love you too.' That was the beginning: what it meant to the hopeless cloistered invalid she told him later—'I had done with living, I thought, when you came and sought me out.'

The famous love story is too well known to need re-telling; its course can be read in the *Sonnets from the Portuguese*—her gift to him—and in the letters the lovers exchanged during the year and half of courtship—letters which, as Chesterton has said, however often published, will still remain private. Owing to her father's opposition they were secretly married in St. Marylebone Church on 12 September, 1846, and a few days later fled to Italy with two companions—Flush, Mrs. Browning's spaniel, and Wilson, her faithful maid. They settled first at Pisa, and then moved to Florence to the Casa Guidi, a house near the Pitti Palace which became their permanent home and where their son was born in 1850. Summers they usually spent among the mountains at Bagni di Lucca and winters occasionally in Rome. As Mrs. Browning's health permitted, they took part in the social and artistic life of Florence and Rome and made friends among the cosmopolitan society of their adopted country; both of them were in strong sympathy with the Italian people who were then feeling the first stirrings of the Risorgimento. During these years Browning produced his finest work, the two volumes of *Men and Women* (1855), *Dramatis Personae* (1862), and *The Ring and the Book* (1868); the latter poem though not written till after his return to England belongs in conception and spirit to the Italian period. Widely as his imagination ranges in these volumes, there are two dominant notes, devotion to his wife and devotion to Italy both in its historic past and active present.

Mrs. Browning died in 1861 and was buried in Florence;

Browning left the city never to return, and came back to England with his son. 'Pen' Browning was ultimately to become an artist of erratic talent, and to him we owe some striking portraits of his father in later years; but his education and upbringing were not without trials and worries for the poet as the boy grew up. Browning was now immediately occupied with the composition of *The Ring and the Book*, which he completed in 1868. This great work, unlike any other long poem of the century, is the climax of his literary career but far from the end of it. The twenty years that still lay ahead were active years both in writing and in social life. His reputation was established, and he was ready to enjoy the rewards of fame. The universities of Oxford and Cambridge conferred honorary degrees and Balliol College made him an Honorary Fellow. The poet, who had not had a university education himself, enjoyed academic society, and came often to Oxford to stay with Jowett at Balliol. The Master once remarked to Florence Nightingale that Browning was the only poet he had known who was also a man of common sense; he may have been thinking of his troubles with a younger Balliol poet, Swinburne, when he said that.[1] In London the Browning Society was founded in his honour in 1881, under the presidency of the Shakespearean scholar F. J. Furnivall. The social lion was now in demand by every important hostess, and the young Henry James wondered how this indefatigable diner-out could be the same person as the poet he admired. His short story *The Private Life* is devoted to that problem. Nevertheless Browning went on writing with unflagging energy and a new volume appeared nearly every year. Inevitably much of this late work has lost the freshness of his best poetry; mannerisms grow and the voice becomes long-winded and argumentative. Yet there are still great moments and many of

[1] Browning expressed his gratitude to Balliol by leaving to the College the manuscripts of all his later poems and various personal relics, including his wedding ring and the Old Yellow Book.

the lyrics show few signs of failing power in an ageing writer.

After the final collected edition of his work in seventeen volumes had appeared in 1889, Browning made his last journey to Italy in the autumn of that year. He visited Asolo again, where he had acquired a property, and then moved to Venice to stay with Pen and his wife, who had settled in the Palazzo Rezzonico on the Grand Canal. Walking on the Lido in late November he caught a chill which developed into a fatal illness, and he died in Venice on 12 December. *Asolando*, his final volume, was published in London on the day before his death, and before the end he had the satisfaction of hearing by telegraph from his publishers the news of its favourable reception. His body was brought home to receive his last honour, burial in the Poets' Corner in Westminster Abbey, on the eve of the New Year. His long life spans the century. He was born when he might still have seen his earliest idols Byron and Shelley plain; when he died the Victorian age was all but over.

III

EARLY POEMS
AND DRAMATIC MONOLOGUES

Like many a young writer whose powers are not yet
equal to his ambitions, Browning was not afraid to embark
on large-scale works. *Pauline*, his first poem, is the not
unfamiliar confession of a young poet in revolt against the
accepted beliefs of his elders. It lays bare more of his inmost
feelings than pleased Browning in later years, when he
republished it with reluctance; its conventions are romantic
and the debt to Shelley obvious, but the signs of a genuine
poet are there, particularly in descriptive passages. In the
next two poems he deals with characters in remote times,
finding in *Paracelsus* a hero in the world of alchemy and
astrology, and in *Sordello* one among the troubadours.
In both poems he was exploring the past through the
medium of books, and not yet living with his creations in
their own age, the faculty which was to become his supreme
gift. It is hard to discover what *Sordello* is about, and thanks
to it Browning early acquired the reputation for obscurity
which he took long to shake off. Tennyson remarked that
there were only two comprehensible lines in it—the first
and the last—and that both were a lie. A glance at the
beginning and at the end of the poem will make clear the
point of the joke.[1] *Pippa Passes* is a different matter. Browning
now leaves the past to tell the story of the little silk-weaver
of Asolo. With her songs she unconsciously influences the
lives of all whose path she crosses on her one happy day
of freedom in the year. He is here writing of a scene that
he knew, and though the plan of these loosely connected
episodes may be artificial the central idea is dramatic
and the heroine herself is not sentimental. Pippa is a first
sketch for the portrait of radiant innocence he was to

[1] Who will, may hear Sordello's story told;

Who would, has heard Sordello's story told.

18

achieve in Pompilia. It is unfortunate that many who
know little else of Browning know her song, and applying
it to his work as a whole charge him with easy uncritical
optimism:

> The year's at the spring
> And day's at the morn;
> Morning's at seven;
> The hill-side's dew-pearled:
> The lark's on the wing,
> The snail's on the thorn;
> God's in his heaven—
> All's right with the world.

This is the whole of Pippa's philosophy but it is only a
part of Browning's: a poem, or part of a poem, can only
be rightly judged in its setting.

The stage plays are, as a whole, failures. To be successful
on the stage poetic drama must possess theatrical life as well
as poetry, and, with possible recent exceptions, its secret has
been lost since the Elizabethan age. Browning's plots are
melodramatic and his characters, despite some fine verse,
fail to come alive in the easy natural flow of dialogue and
in the interplay of motive and action. He can be truly
dramatic when he sets himself to deal with a single figure
in reflective or argumentative mood, and for this he found
the right vehicle not on the stage but in the dramatic
monologue, a form he has made peculiarly his own. The
happiest result of this association with Macready was not
the plays but the poem he wrote to amuse the actor's small
son during an illness:

> So, Willy, let you and me be wipers
> Of scores out with all men—especially pipers:
> And, whether they pipe us free, from rats or from mice,
> If we promised them aught, let us keep our promise.

The Pied Piper of Hamelin, with its excitement and fantasy
and right kind of moral for childhood, is a high success
in a kind of poetry where success is rare. It has delighted
many children since.

The monologue was popular, and Browning is only one of many Victorian writers who used it; a glance at one of Tennyson's monologues will show by contrast what is distinctive in Browning's handling of the form. In *Ulysses* Tennyson depicts a great figure in a moment of resolve. It is a noble reflective poem but it is not dramatic; there is no movement and the scene is barely indicated. Though the hero holds the stage alone we feel him a voice rather than see him as a presence, and the minor characters are shadows: a third dimension is lacking. The oarsmen are only there to strike the sounding furrow at the right moment. Compare them with the rippling muscled sailors who unload the ship in Browning's *Cleon*. In Browning's monologues every detail of the setting tells, and his tiny stage is peopled with fully rounded figures though only the main character has the speaking part. When the dying Bishop orders his tomb, we see and feel the jasper, the peach-bloom marble, and the lapis 'blue as a vein in the Madonna's breast'; his three thankless sons are present, and we watch the hated rival Gandolf still spying from his niche as he did in life. While Fra Lippo talks, the rough soldier faces flicker round him in the torch-light, and the pattering feet of the 'lights of love' echo in the distance. As Andrea ponders on his failure and unrealized ambitions in the darkening studio, he is not alone; his wife Lucrezia emerges from the shadows to wait for the signal from the cousin-lover waiting outside. These are scenes which grow in depth; in each there is action rising to climax as the characters interact and develop. Irony is used to point the situation, and there is always an intellectual problem, stated or implied, to give a motive to the piece. This is the art of dramatic monologue as practised by a Ruth Draper and its other great exponents on the stage. With the enlarging power of poetry Browning extends its range and uses it for an infinite variety of imaginative creations. 'The utterances of so many imaginary persons, not mine'; so he described the monologues to his friend Milsand, but his own voice is heard too:

> Love, you saw me gather men and women,
> Live or dead or fashioned by my fancy,
> Enter each and all, and use their service,
> Speak from every mouth—the speech a poem.[1]

The early monologue, *The Bishop orders his Tomb at St. Praxed's Church*, which was inspired by the poet's visit to the church of Santa Prassede in Rome in 1848, already shows his full mastery of the form. Ruskin, whose words deserve to be quoted in full, said that it caught more of the Renaissance spirit than he had been able to put into pages of *The Stones of Venice*.[2] The Bishop is the embodiment of Renaissance worldliness and luxury, while the Grammarian in another poem represents the austere and self-denying discipline of the revival of learning. There is a nice irony in the contrast. The Grammarian, 'loftier living, loftier dying', leaves an enduring memorial in the spirit of devotion he has kindled in the disciples who bear his body to its last resting-place on the mountain-top. The Bishop who has lived for the things of this world perishes with them: for we know that the graceless sons will not respect his wishes and the cherished tomb will be no more than a dying man's dream:

> For as I lie here, hours of the dead night,
> Dying in state and by such slow degrees,
> I fold my arms as if they clasped a crook,
> And stretch my feet forth straight as stone can point,
> And let the bed clothes, for a mort-cloth, drop
> Into great laps and folds of sculptor's work . . .
> . . . There, leave me, there;
> For ye have stabbed me with ingratitude
> To death—ye wish it—God, ye wish it! Stone—
> Gritstone, a-crumble! Clammy squares which sweat

---

[1] *One Word More.*

[2] 'I know of no other piece of modern English prose or poetry, in which there is so much told of the Renaissance spirit—its worldliness, inconsistency, pride, hypocrisy, ignorance of itself, love of art, of luxury, and of Good Latin. It is nearly all that I have said of the central Renaissance in thirty pages of the *Stones of Venice*, Browning's also being the antecedent work' (*Modern Painters*, IV, 380).

As if the corpse they keep were oozing through—
And no more *lapis* to delight the world!
Well, go! I bless ye. Fewer tapers there,
But in a row; and, going, turn your backs
—Ay, like departing altar-ministrants,
And leave me in my church, the church for peace,
That I may watch at leisure if he leers—
Old Gandolf, at me, from his onion stone,
As still he envied me, so fair she was!

The great monologues of the middle years which are to be found in *Men and Women* and in *Dramatis Personae* range far and wide in theme. In *Fra Lippo Lippi*, Browning uses a knowledge of early Florentine painting rare in an Englishman of that time to illustrate an enduring problem of art. Brother Lippo escaping for a night from the restrictions of his monastery is caught by the city watch at the alley's end:

I could not paint all night—
Ouf! I leaned out of window for fresh air.
There came a hurry of feet, and little feet,
A sweep of lute-strings, laughs, and whifts of song.
Flower o' the broom,
Take away love, and our earth is a tomb!

With a few quick strokes the scene is set, the character outlined, and the all too human Lippo proceeds to tell the story of his life, from its start as ragamuffin starving in the streets of Florence to his present employment as monastic painter. The moral, or the problem, which gives a motive to the piece is the question of reconciling two opposing forces in religious art—the flesh and the spirit:

Your business is to paint the souls of men . . .
Give us no more of body than shows soul!
Here's Giotto, with his Saint a-praising God!
That sets you praising—why not stop with him?
Why put all thoughts of praise out of our heads
With wonder at lines, colours, and what not?
Paint the soul, never mind the legs and arms!
Rub all out, try at it a second time.

That is the Prior's view, but young Lippo cannot stop with
Giotto:

> Why can't a painter lift each foot in turn,
> Left foot and right foot, go a double step,
> Make his flesh liker, and his soul more like
> Both in their order? . . .
> The beauty and the wonder and the power,
> The shapes of things, their colours, lights and shades,
> Changes, surprises—and God made it all!

And then we hear Browning's own voice:

> The world's no blot for us,
> Nor blank—it means intensely, and means good:
> To find its meaning is my meat and drink.

The poem is full of life and movement and humour and
snatches of song, and it poses a question every reader can
understand. It was a favourite with its author, and he used
often to read it aloud. On one memorable evening when
the Brownings were in London in 1855, there was a gather-
ing of poets in their rooms in Dorset Street. Tennyson read
his newly published *Maud* the tears coursing down his
cheeks, and Browning followed with *Fra Lippo Lippi*;
meanwhile Rossetti unobserved made a pen and ink sketch
of the scene.[1]

In *Andrea del Sarto* he takes another subject from Italian
art. This speaking picture of the 'faultless painter' and his
wife was written for the poet's friend John Kenyon, who had
asked for a copy of the supposed portrait of Andrea and
Lucrezia in the Pitti Gallery. Here the hopes and ambitions
of youth have yielded to the sad acceptance of age.
Browning called it his 'twilight piece'; it is a nocturne and
the tones are silver grey:

> A common greyness silvers everything—
> All in a twilight you and I alike.
> —You, at the point of your first pride in me,

[1] Several versions of this drawing exist; one is in the Birmingham City
Art Gallery.

(That's gone you know)—but I, at every point;
My youth, my hope, my art, being all toned down
To yonder sober pleasant Fiesole . . .
The last monk leaves the garden; days decrease
And autumn grows, autumn in everything.

The tragedy of this study of failure lies in the resignation:

Ah, but a man's reach should exceed his grasp,
Or what's a heaven for?

What Browning felt about 'the unlit lamp and ungirt loin'
he lets us know in *The Statue and the Bust*, where he is
speaking in his own person: in *Andrea* the dramatic artist is
too wise to step in and point a moral. He lets the mood he
has evoked speak for itself; it is his faultless monologue.

We can do no more than indicate the range and variety of
these volumes. Two monologues in the form of epistle
examine the Christian hope of immortality as seen by
cultured observers in the pagan world. *Cleon* voices the
despair of a Greek poet approaching the end of life in the
Hellenistic age; *An Epistle of Karshish* tells of the meeting of
an Arab physician with Lazarus whom Christ has raised
from the dead. Cleon rejects the Christian hope and the
message of St. Paul with all the scorn of the cultivated
Greek mind:

Thou canst not think a mere barbarian Jew,
As Paulus proves to be, one circumcised,
Hath access to a secret shut from us?
Thou wrongest our philosophy, O king.

Karshish the wiser scientific enquirer does not close his
mind to evidence of belief because it is undreamt of in his
philosophy:

The very God! think, Abid; dost thou think?
So, the All-Great, were the All-Loving too—

This poem is also a remarkable exercise in the historic irony
of time:

Alas! it grieveth me, the learned leech
Perished in a tumult many years ago,

Accused—our learning's fate—of wizardry.
Rebellion, to the setting up a rule
And creed prodigious as described to me.
His death which happened when the earthquake fell
Was wrought by the mad people—that's their wont.

It is the device used so successfully by Anatole France when dealing with a similar theme in his short story *The Procurator of Judea*.

In the famous *Bishop Bloughram's Apology* where Browning took Cardinal Wiseman as his model, he presents theological argument in a contemporary setting. This brilliant piece of casuistry, semi-serious, semi-flippant, allows the Bishop to justify the Catholic position in argument with the agnostic journalist Gigadibs. Gigadibs never speaks, but he is there to the life, taking his wine, making his points, and losing his case. Even in abstruse argument Browning will break into poetry somewhere; he does it here in 'the sunset-touch and chorus ending from Euripides'. He turns to contemporary life again in *Mr. Sludge 'the Medium'*, a long and bitter attack on spiritualism and its adherents. The victim is one Home, a popular medium of the time, in whom Mrs. Browning displayed an interest. The poet had attended one of his séances with some sense of conviction, but later came to resent Home's influence on his wife, and personal feeling colours the attack. But over and above the personal resentment a consuming anger is directed at the trickery which under the guise of comfort would traffic in human grief. Browning was tolerant of many failings but he felt as strongly about meanness and hypocrisy as Shakespeare and Dickens did.

IV

OTHER POEMS

During these early and middle years Browning wrote much in kinds other than the monologue and long poem; 'poems of all sorts and sizes and styles and subjects', and from these space again allows us only to select and indicate. *Rabbi Ben Ezra* and *Childe Roland to the Dark Tower Came* are well known, the one an expression of confidence in life lived to the full with the increasing wisdom of age, the other a great utterance of courage set in the nightmare region of dream and fantasy. There are awkward patches in the poems, perverse lines which flaunt the irritating tricks of his style. But for all that Browning is a master of metre and inventive in stanza forms. There is writing of a different kind in the quiet music of *Love among the Ruins*, in the swing of *The Last Ride Together*, and in the long lyric sweep of *Saul*. In his love poetry there is passion, simple and direct, as well as thought. With all his manly vigour there was a feminine strain in his nature, inherited no doubt from his early upbringing, but he avoids the mawkish and sentimental which is so often the weakness of Victorian love poetry.

Many English poets espoused the cause of Italian freedom but few wrote of it with more personal feeling than Browning. Both he and his wife felt the early stages of the struggle to be their own cause. He writes not in general political terms from a world point of view, but as a man on the spot who understands the feelings of the humblest peasant. *The Italian in England* gives a noble picture of a 'contadina' in the north who is loyal to the betrayed fugitive she has discovered—'in calm simplicity of grace, our Italy's own attitude'. This was the poem Mazzini read aloud to cheer the disheartened Italian exiles in London. The intensity of hatred in the lines:

> I would grasp Metternich until
> I felt his wet red throat distil
> In blood thro' these two hands.

is a feminine touch; it was supplied by Mrs. Browning. In *De Gustibus* the scene changes to the Bourbon kingdom of Naples. Somewhere along that 'great opaque blue breadth of sea' a bare-foot peasant girl tumbles the flesh-green melons down on the pavement:

> And says there's news today—the king
> Was shot at, touched in the liver-wing,
> Goes with his Bourbon arm in a sling:
> —She hopes they have not caught the felons.

Old Pictures in Florence combines this theme whimsically with his love and knowledge of the early Italian masters.

> 'Robert (wrote Mrs. Browning in 1850) has been picking up pictures at a few pauls each, "hole and corner" pictures which the dealers had not found out . . . one of the best judges in Florence throws out such names for them as Cimabue, Ghirlandajo, Giottino, a crucifixion painted on a banner, Giottesque, if not Giotto, but *unique*, or nearly so.'

The fading panels and peeling frescoes, says the poem, will come to life again when the Austrian yoke is thrown off, and Giotto's unfinished bell-tower will then rise to its full height, the symbol of united Italy:

> And fine as the beak of a young beccaccia
> The Campanile, the Duomo's fit ally,
> Soars up in gold its full fifty braccia,
> Completing Florence as Florence Italy.

In these poems of the middle years, the Italian landscape is ever-present in the background and with it the companion-ship of his wife. *Two in the Campagna* paints the pair in the still unspoiled country around Rome; *By the Fireside* moves from the Tuscan hills in summer, to glimpse the intimate autumn interior at Casa Guidi:

> And to watch you sink by the fire side now,
> Back again, as you mutely sit
> Musing by firelight, that great brow
> And the spirit-small hand propping it,
> Yonder, my heart knows how!

The most moving of all his tributes to Mrs. Browning is the poem he wrote in grief after her death, a poem which gives expression to his own dauntless courage. *Prospice* is the forerunner of the *Epilogue* which was to be his own epitaph, and it is the finer poem:

> I was ever a fighter, so—one fight more,
>   The best and the last!
> I would hate that death bandaged my eyes, and forebore,
>   And bade me creep past.
> No! let me taste the whole of it, fare like my peers
>   The heroes of old,
> Bear the brunt in a minute pay glad life's arrears
>   Of pain, darkness and cold.
> For sudden the worst turns best to the brave,
>   The black minute's at end,
> And the elements rage, the fiend-voices that rave,
>   Shall dwindle, shall blend,
> Shall change, shall become first a peace out of pain,
>   Then a light, then thy breast,
> O thou soul of my soul! I shall clasp thee again,
>   And with God be the rest!

V

THE RING AND THE BOOK

At the beginning of his greatest poem *The Ring and the Book*, Browning tells how one blazing June day of 1860 he found 'the square old yellow book' on a stall in the market of San Lorenzo in Florence, and for a lira made it his:

> Across a square in Florence, crammed with booths,
> Buzzing and blaze, noontide and market time . . .
> 'Mongst odds and ends of ravage, picture-frames
> White through the worn gilt, mirror-sconces chipped,
> Bronze angel-heads once knobs attached to chests,
> (Handled when ancient dames chose forth brocade)
> Modern chalk drawings, studies from the nude,
> Samples of stone, jet, breccia, porphry . . .
> From these . . . Oh, with a Lionard going cheap
> If it should prove, as promised, that Joconde
> Whereof a copy contents the Louvre!—these
> I picked this book from. Five compeers in flank
> Stood left and right of it as tempting more—
> With this, one glance at the lettered back of which,
> And 'Stall!' cried I: a *lira* made it mine.

The passage, too long to quote in full, catches that typical Florentine scene in all its colour and with it the very pathos and poetry of debris. The find was an account of a forgotten murder trial which took place in Rome in the seventeenth century; pure crude fact:

> Secreted from man's life when hearts beat hard,
> And brains, high-blooded, ticked two centuries hence.

In brief, the documents told how the impoverished Count Guido Franceschini of Arezzo, having been tricked in his marriage to the secretly adopted daughter of a childless Roman couple Pietro and Violante Comparini, by his cruelty and persecution drove her to leave his house. She was helped in her flight to Rome by a young priest the Canon Caponsacchi. Accusing her of infidelity Guido murdered his girl-wife and her supposed parents in circumstances of the utmost brutality. Then when handed over to justice he appealed from the civil court of Rome to the Pope, and by him was found guilty and condemned to death. Unpromising material for poetry, but the violent tale with its strong contrasts of good and evil fired Browning's imagination, and the fascination grew as he unravelled the tangled web, following legal case and counter-case in pursuit of the truth. The poem which finally appeared in 1868 had been growing in his mind ever since the discovery of the old yellow book, though it was not written till his return to England after Mrs. Browning's death. It is in fact the last great memorial of the Italian years, and it is also his wife's poem:

> O lyric Love, half angel and half bird
> And all a wonder and a wild desire, . . .
> Hail then, and hearken from the realms of help!
> Never may I commence my song, my due
> To God who best taught song by gift of thee,
> Except with bent head and beseeching hand—
> That still, despite the distance and the dark,
> What was, again may be; some interchange
> Of grace, some splendour once thy very thought,
> Some benediction anciently thy smile!

It is dedicated to her memory; the ring, symbol of truth, is her ring; and the warmth and tenderness shown in the portrayal of the heroine is a tribute to her too.

The story is presented in a series of monologues. This form which Browning had practised and perfected was the inevitable vehicle, for it was not the story which attracted him so much as the character and motives of the participants. Yet *The Ring and The Book* is more than another collection of separate monologues; it has the organic shape and unity of a great work and this is achieved by the well-considered placing and relationship of its parts. It is an architectural whole carefully planned, and a grasp of the vast ground plan will make the reading easier.

The first book is introductory, deliberately personal and miscellaneous; in it the poet explains the significance of the title, outlines the different situations, and concludes with the invocation to his wife. In a similar way the final book gathers up loose ends and fades the old woe back into time. The intervening ten books fall into groups related by points of climax and contrast. We are given the outline of the story at the start; it is told and retold from various angles and the excitement consists, as in a certain kind of detective story, in hearing the evidence and finding the clues which will lead to the truth.

The poem proper opens in the second book with the description of the stabbed bodies of the murdered Comparini pair—and the dying Pompilia so soon to join them—displayed to view in the Church of San Lorenzo in Lucina; all Rome crowds in to the sight and takes sides according to what it knew of one party or the other. Browning, by a brilliant stroke, invents a character to speak for the One Half Rome who are on Guido's side, followed by another to represent the Other Half Rome who support Pompilia. Then a Tertium Quid—no gossip guess of the people he, but the cold cynical and would-be authoritative voice of upper Roman society. With these three books the prologue is over; we have heard the story as Rome sees it and are now eager to hear the chief actors speak for themselves. First Guido, making an able case before his judges for the wronged husband who seeks to justify his crime as an act of rightful revenge committed in hot blood. How much of it can we believe? Next Caponsacchi, the rescuer and supposed lover, testifying fearlessly to Pompilia's innocence and to his own: generous honesty following Guido's cold craft? Then the dying Pompilia's confession, telling of the bitter wrongs she has suffered, of hope restored by the 'soldier saint' her rescuer, and humbly thankful for one brief glimpse of peace and happiness with her new-born babe. Never did Browning write with greater tenderness and pathos; he idealizes the figure he found in the source-book, but makes us believe in her courage and radiant innocence as profoundly as did the friar who heard her dying words.

Now there is a pause in the action as this point of climax is reached, and Browning fills it with the pleadings of the two lawyers arguing on either side. These two books may be regarded as the scherzo or lighter movement of a great symphony, or as the so-called 'comic relief' of Elizabethan tragedy—a deliberate easing of tension before the action mounts again to climax. True it is a malicious kind of relief, for the poet indulges himself in much legal Latin and in a bravura display of 'Ovidian quip and Ciceronian crank'; but however much they may puzzle the reader the purpose of these two books in the dramatic scheme is plain enough.

We are still in suspense about the result of Guido's appeal to the Pope, and with the Pope's judgement in the tenth book the poem rises to its supreme heights. The aged Innocent XII, as he reviews the case through the length of a sombre winter day in the silent Vatican, is a grand, austere, yet human and believable figure. In him Browning has created a character who can give utterance to the poet's own criticism of life and voice his profoundest thoughts on the mystery of sin and suffering and man's responsibility in the world:

> White shall not neutralize the black; nor good
> Compensate bad in man, absolve him so:
> Life's business being just the terrible choice.

Finally we see Guido once more when he learns his doom. We have already seen him as he wanted his judges and the world to see him: now on the night before execution, with soul stripped bare, he reveals the true self, pitiless in cruelty, greed and pride. The curtain falls on a last terrible and unrepentant cry of self-abasing despair:

> Abate—Cardinal—Christ—Maria—God, . . .
> Pompilia, will you let them murder me?

Thus the separate parts of the poem are interlocked; each retelling has added some fresh detail and thrown some new light on fact, till finally the truth is reached. A bold and original architectural scheme has been carried through and this great poem is as unique in shape as it is in content.

Browning has successfully avoided the temptation of making his characters abstract types; they are live embodiments of good and evil, or those 'sadly mixed natures somewhere twixt the best and worst'. Guido is rivalled only by Iago in breathing villainy. Pompilia is drawn with pathos unmarred by sentimentality, and through suffering the girl-wife grows to mature womanhood before our eyes. The Pope who is the poet's mouthpiece at the same time exists in his own right, and is presented as a great humane pontiff of history. For him and for certain other figures the poet found little or no material to build on in the source-book. The sheer power of his creative imagination is shown in the shaping of the three voices of Rome, the two lawyers, and Caponsacchi, out of a mere hint or name. The minor characters, who fill the background of this vast canvas, are no less real than the main actors. As an instance of his skill in character drawing take the Abate Paolo's visit to Violante for the purpose of baiting the hook which will secure Pompilia for his brother:

> So—giving now his great flap-hat a gloss
> With flat o' the hand between whiles, smoothing now
> The silk from out its creases o'er the calf,
> Setting the stocking clerical again,
> But never disengaging, once engaged,
> The thin clear grey hold of his eyes on her.

This is the mastery of significant detail that Chaucer was the first to teach. It is by like observation of telling historical and social detail that Browning brings the setting to life. We live with these people the life of *seicento* Rome; we join them in church and theatre, jostle with the crowd in the Corso, and make our way at the end of carnival to the People's Square, where the dread knife 'Mannaia' is awaiting Guido led to execution by the Company of Death.

The poem is written in a free-running blank verse which in movement and diction often recalls the late Shakespearean line. No poem of such a length is without its flat passages; there are times when too much is said, and times when the verse crosses the boundary which divides poetry from prose. But Browning can pull it back to safety with a descriptive touch; as in the picture of those 'stout tall bright-eyed and black-haired boys' who labour in Guido's Tuscan vineyard:

> Are these i' the mood to murder, hardly loosed
> From healthy autumn finish, the ploughed glebe,
> Grapes in the barrel, work at happy end,
> And winter come with rest and Christmas play?

He was writing for the last time on the grand scale and at the height of his powers. The dark tale relived was a challenge to formulate his interpretation of life, and he meets it by stating once again the belief which is the basis of all his work:

> Life is probation and this earth no goal
> But starting-point of man.

His faith and philosophy break through the darkness of the storm in the great revealing flash of the Pope's last utterance:

> I stood at Naples once, a night so dark
> I could have scarce conjectured there was earth
> Anywhere, sky, or sea or world at all:
> But the night's black was burst through by a blaze—
> Thunder struck blow on blow, earth groaned and bore,
> Through her length of mountain visible:
> There lay the city thick and plain with spires,
> And, like a ghost disshrouded, white the sea,
> So may the truth be flashed out by one blow,
> And Guido see, one instant, and be saved.
> Else I avert my face, nor follow him
> Into that sad obscure sequestered state
> Where God unmakes, but to remake the soul
> He else first made in vain; which must not be.

VI

LATE POEMS AND CONCLUSION

During the remaining twenty years of his life—years of fame and busy social activity, Browning wrote on with unabated energy, bringing out volume after volume. Much of this late work will not appeal to every Browning lover. Fluency had become a habit, and almost any subject would now serve for a poem. The eccentricities of style grow more marked, and though the intellectual energy is immense we often feel that head is working at expense of heart. There are writers and painters in whose later work difficulty of style and unconventionality are the signs of deepening emotion and profounder wisdom, the evidences of a new vision. But this is hardly the case with Browning. An assertive note can be heard even in self-parody, and there are occasional moments of ill-temper.

> The bard's a Browning; he neglects the form;
> But ah, the sense, ye Gods, the weighty sense.

Yet he is still capable of great things, and in lyric inspiration can write with all the warmth and passion of youth. It would be hard to guess that some of the shorter poems of this period are the work of a man nearing his seventies.

> Out of your whole life give but a moment!
> All of your life that has gone before,
> All to come after it—so you ignore
> So you make perfect the present—condense,
> In a rapture of rage, for perfection's endowment,
> Thought and feeling and soul and sense—
> Merged in a moment which gives me at last
> You around me for once, you beneath me, above me—
> Me—sure that despite of time future, time past—
> This tick of our life-time's one moment you love me!
> How long such suspension may linger? Ah, Sweet—
> The moment eternal—just that and no more—

> When ecstasy's utmost we clutch at the core
> While cheeks burn, arms open, eyes shut and lips meet! [1]

In other late lyrics this lambent flame fades and sinks into the reflective contentment of age. He can now look for the last time on the beloved Asolo of his youth with different wiser eyes:

> The Poet's age is sad: for why?
>   In youth, the natural world could show
> No common object but his eye
>   At once involved with alien glow—
> His own soul's iris-bow.
>
> .   .   .
>
> How many a year my Asolo,
>   Since—one step just from sea to land—
> I found you, loved yet feared you so—
>   For natural objects seemed to stand
> Palpably fire clothed! No—
>
> And now? The lambent flame is—where?
>   Lost from the naked world; earth, sky,
> Hill, vale, tree, flower—Italia's rare
>   O'er running beauty crowds the eye—
> But flame? The Bush is bare.
>
> No, for the purged ear apprehends
>   Earth's import, not the eye late dazed;
> The Voice said 'Call my works thy friends'.
>   At Nature dost thou shrink amazed?
> God is it who transcends.

Among the longer poems *Fifine at the Fair* strikes a note that is heard more than once in the later volumes. The hero Don Juan walks through the fair with Elvire the perfect wife, but is drawn away from her by the attractions of the wayward and beautiful gipsy Fifine. This poem was written after he had proposed marriage to Lady Ashburton in 1869 and been rejected. It clearly reflects a mood occasioned by that experience, but it is more of an intellectual

[1] *Now.*

exercise than a personal story. The hero refines on his problem interminably with copious and unending flow of argument and illustration: yet there is characterisitic poetry in the similes and in the descriptions of the Breton country round Pornic, where the poet used to spend his summers with his son. Browning felt the need of feminine companion-ship in his solitary years, and he had many happy friend-ships with women. But the memory of his dead wife remained, and her shade troubles some of this later love poetry, as it does in the strange and powerful *St. Martin's Summer*:

> Ghosts! O breathing Beauty,
>   Give me frank word pardon!
>   What if I—somehow, somewhere—
> Pledged my soul to endless duty
>   Many a time and oft? Be hard on
>   Love—laid there?

A renewed study of the Greek dramatists gave him the inspiration for two poems which are a defence of Euripides against modern detractors. The graceful *Balaustion's Adventure* tells how a band of Athenian exiles won refuge at Syracuse by chanting the poetry of Euripides to their captors. The version of the *Alcestis* which is part of it is a tribute to the Greek dramatist who had been Mrs. Browning's favourite poet, and in whom Browning himself found a questioning genius akin to his own. The heroine Balaustion is one of his finest female portraits and in her he recaptures the spirit of an Athens as yet untamed by Spartan tyranny. There is less poetry in the sequel, *Aristophanes Apologizes*, which suffers from excessive length and an indulgence in crabbed allusions to the technicalities of Greek diction and metre. Browning however discerns the grave face beneath the comic mask of the satiric dramatist:

> A sea worn face, sad as mortality,
> Divine with yearning after fellowship.

He lets Aristophanes make a magnificent defence of his art which states the serious function of comedy in literature and life as well as that has ever been done. He turns from Greece to imperial Rome to pose once more the old problem of Christianity breaking into a pagan world; *Imperante Augusto natus est* presents it for the last time with all the old historical imagination undimmed. These poems will serve to indicate the strength and the weakness of the late Browning. The reader who would explore further is referred to the full list of works in the bibliography.

Browning with all his range is a consistent poet. Vigour of mind and warmth of heart mark the man from first to last. His chief interest is always in human beings, whose problems he examines with an intellect that is keen and stimulating. Instead of thinking for the reader he makes the reader think for himself, and that is why he has acquired his reputation for difficulty. He will jerk us to attention with a strange word, a fantastic rhyme or with the sharp voice of humour and common sense. The vast unconventional vocabulary, the wide reading, the wealth of allusion, the intellectual curiosity—these are things that do not make for easy reading, but we accept them when we realize that they are not affectation but a live part of the poet's experience. It is by means of them that he can project himself into the past and relive it. His historical poems are never mere costume pieces; the men and women, past and present, speak convincingly with the accents of their own age. He lacks the verbal magic of a Tennyson; his vigour can degenerate into roughness and his learning into obscurity. Sometimes for not keeping the accent he deserves to be hanged, but, like Donne, of whom he was an early admirer, he can also write as musically as the best of his contemporaries: he was indeed a master of metre as skilled as any of them. His poetry squarely faces the evil and the inexplicable in existence; the optimism and faith which are his answer to them remain unimpaired because they are based not on assertive self-confidence but ultimately on humility. In almost his last poem he can write:

> I have faith such end shall be:
>   From the first, Power was—I knew.
> Life has made clear to me
>   That strive but for closer view,
> Love were as plain to see.

With all his failings he is honest, warm-hearted, and human, and he was a fighter to the end:

> One who never turned his back but marched breast forward,
>   Never doubted clouds would break,
> Never dreamed, though right were worsted, wrong would triumph,
>   Held we fall to rise, are baffled to fight better,
>   Sleep to wake.

It is told that when he was reading the proofs of *Asolando* on the eve of his last illness he paused and said of that verse of the *Epilogue*—'it almost sounds like bragging to say this, and as if I ought to cancel it; but it's the simple truth, and as it's true it shall stand'.

ROBERT BROWNING
A Select Bibliography
(Place of publication London, unless stated otherwise)

Bibliographies:

A GUIDE BOOK TO THE POETIC AND DRAMATIC WORKS, by G. W. Cooke. Boston (1891).

A COMPLETE BIBLIOGRAPHY OF THE WRITINGS IN PROSE AND VERSE, by T. J. Wise (1897).

A BROWNING LIBRARY, by T. J. Wise (1929).
A catalogue of the Browning collection in the Ashley Library, now in the British Museum.

ROBERT BROWNING: A BIBLIOGRAPHY 1830–1950, by L. N. Broughton, C. S. Northup and R. Pearsall. Ithaca (1953).

Note: Useful material will be found in the Browning Society's Papers, edited by F. J. Furnivall (1881–1891), and in Baylor University's Browning Interests Series, edited by A. J. Armstrong, Waco, Texas, 1927–49.

Collected Works:

POEMS. 2 vols. (1849); 3 vols. (1863); 6 vols. (1868).

THE POETICAL WORKS, 17 vols. (1888–94).
This edition contains the author's final arrangement of his poems and revisions of his texts.

THE POETICAL WORKS, edited by A. Birrell and F. G. Kenyon. 2 vols. (1896).

THE COMPLETE WORKS (the Florentine Edition), edited by C. Porter and H. A. Clarke. 12 vols. New York (1898).

THE WORKS (the Centenary Edition), edited by F. G. Kenyon. 10 vols. (1912).

THE COMPLETE POETICAL WORKS, edited by A. Birrell. 2 vols. (1919).
THE POEMS AND PLAYS. New York (1934).
In the Modern Library.

Selections:

SELECTIONS FROM THE POETICAL WORKS (1884).
The poet's own choice.

POEMS AND PLAYS, 4 vols. (1906).
In Everyman's Library. New edition, 1956, with a general introduction by J. Bryson.

THE POETICAL WORKS COMPLETE FROM 1833–1868, AND THE SHORTER POEMS THEREAFTER. Oxford (1940).
In the Oxford Standard Authors series.

POEMS, edited by H. Milford. Oxford (1949).
In the World's Classics series.

POETRY AND PROSE, selected by S. Nowell Smith (1950).
In the Reynard Library.

Separate Works:

PAULINE: A FRAGMENT OF A CONFESSION (1833).

PARACELSUS (1835).

STRAFFORD: AN HISTORICAL TRAGEDY (1837).

SORDELLO (1840).

BELLS AND POMEGRANATES, 8 parts (1841–46).
No. i Pippa Passes. 1841.
No. ii King Victor and King Charles. 1842.
No. iii Dramatic Lyrics. 1842.
No. iv The Return of the Druses. A Tragedy. 1843.
No. v A Blot in the Scutcheon. A Tragedy. 1843.
No. vi Colombe's Birthday. A Play. 1844.
No. vii Dramatic Romances and Lyrics. 1845.
No. viii Luria; and A Soul's Tragedy. 1846.
Each part was published separately in paper wrappers under its own title. The series of 8 parts, when complete, was issued in cloth boards with the general title 'Bells and Pomegranates'.

CHRISTMAS EVE AND EASTER DAY. A Poem (1850).

MEN AND WOMEN. 2 vols. (1855).
The separate editions of 'Cleon' and 'The Statue and the Bust' (fraudulently dated 1855) were forged many years later by T. J. Wise.

DRAMATIS PERSONAE (1864).
The separate edition of 'Gold Hair' (1864 *sic*) is another Wise forgery.

THE RING AND THE BOOK. 4 vols. (1868–69).
Edited by E. Dowden, Oxford, 1912.

BALAUSTION'S ADVENTURE (1871).
Edited by E. A. Parker, 1929.

PRINCE HOHENSTIEL-SCHWANGAU, SAVIOUR OF SOCIETY (1871).

FIFINE AT THE FAIR (1872).

RED COTTON NIGHT-CAP COUNTRY OR TURF AND TOWERS (1873).

ARISTOPHANES' APOLOGY (1875).

THE INN ALBUM (1875).

PACCHIAROTTO, AND HOW HE WORKED IN DISTEMPER: WITH OTHER POEMS (1876).

THE AGAMEMNON OF AESCHYLUS (1877).

LA SAISIAZ: THE TWO POETS OF CROISIC (1878).

DRAMATIC IDYLS: First series (1879); Second series (1880).

JOCOSERIA (1883).

FERISHTAH'S FANCIES (1884).

PARLEYINGS WITH CERTAIN PEOPLE OF IMPORTANCE IN THEIR DAY (1887).

ASOLANDO: FANCIES AND FACTS (1890) [1889]

[AN ESSAY ON PERCY BYSSHE SHELLEY (1852).
Written as "Introductory Essay" to a collection of Shelley's Letters issued in 1852, which was suppressed when they were proved to be spurious. The essay, edited by F. J. Furnivall, was reprinted in the first volume of the Browning Society Papers in 1881, and has frequently been reprinted since.]

Letters:

THE LETTERS OF ROBERT BROWNING AND ELIZABETH BARRETT, 1845–46. 2 vols. (1899).

ROBERT BROWNING AND ALFRED DOMETT, edited by F. G. Kenyon (1906).

LETTERS OF ROBERT BROWNING: Collected by T. J. Wise, edited by T. L. Hood. New Haven (1933).
Various groups of letters in this collection had been issued previously in separate privately printed editions.

TWENTY-TWO UNPUBLISHED LETTERS OF E. B. BROWNING AND R. BROWNING TO HENRIETTA AND ARABELLA MOULTON-BARRETT. New York (1935).

FROM ROBERT AND ELIZABETH BROWNING, A FURTHER SELECTION OF THE BARRETT–BROWNING FAMILY CORRESPONDENCE, edited by W. R. Benét (1936).

ROBERT BROWNING AND JULIA WEDGWOOD. A BROKEN FRIENDSHIP AS REVEALED IN THEIR LETTERS, edited by R. Curle (1937).

NEW LETTERS OF ROBERT BROWNING, edited by W. C. de Vane and K. L. Knickerbocker. New Haven (1950).

DEAREST ISA. ROBERT BROWNING'S LETTERS TO ISABELLA BLAGDEN, edited by E. C. McAleer. Austin, Texas (1951).

Some Critical and Biographical Studies:

A HANDBOOK TO THE WORKS, edited by Mrs. Sutherland Orr (1886). Revised edition, 1887.

AN INTRODUCTION TO THE STUDY OF BROWNING, by A. Symons (1886).

ROBERT BROWNING: PERSONALIA, by E. Gosse (1890).

LIFE AND LETTERS OF ROBERT BROWNING, by Mrs. Sutherland Orr (1891).
Revised by F. G. Kenyon 1908.

THE POETRY OF ROBERT BROWNING, by S. A. Brooke (1902); 2 vols. (1905).

THE BROWNING CYCLOPAEDIA, edited by E. Berdoe (1902).

ROBERT BROWNING, by G. K. Chesterton (1903).
In the English Men of Letters series.

LIFE OF ROBERT BROWNING, by E. Dowden (1904).

ROBERT BROWNING, by C. H. Herford (1905).

THE LIFE OF ROBERT BROWNING, WITH NOTICES OF HIS WRITINGS, HIS FAMILY, AND HIS FRIENDS, by W. H. Griffin and H. C. Minchin (1910).
Revised edition 1938.

THE EARLY CAREER OF ROBERT BROWNING, by T. R. Lounsbury (1912).

BROWNING: HOW TO KNOW HIM, by W. L. Phelps (1915).
New enlarged edition 1933.

A COMMENTARY UPON 'THE RING AND THE BOOK', by A. K. Cook (1920).

A CONCORDANCE TO THE POEMS, by L. N. Broughton and B. F. Stelter. 2 vols. New York (1924–25).

THE BROWNINGS, by O. Elton (1924).

THE VERSIFICATION OF ROBERT BROWNING, by H. A. Hatcher. Columbus, Ohio (1928).

SOME MEMORIES OF ROBERT BROWNING BY HIS DAUGHTER-IN-LAW, F. Barrett Browning, Boston (1928).

THE REPUTATION OF ROBERT BROWNING, by D. C. Somervell (1929). In Essays and Studies by Members of the English Association, XV.

THE BROWNINGS, by O. Burdett (1933).

A BROWNING HANDBOOK, by W. C. De Vane. New York (1935). Second edition, revised 1955.

ROBERT BROWNING, A PORTRAIT, by B. Miller (1952).

ROBERT BROWNING, by J. M. Cohen (1952).